Amazon Free Time Unlimited: Your Guide to FreeTime Unlimited Books & Maximizing Your Free Time Unlimited Subscription

Sarah Goldberg

Table of Contents

Introduction To Amazon Free Time Unlimited 4

What is Amazon FreeTime Unlimited? 6

Similar Competitor Services 11

Troubleshooting 16

Subscription Process and Setup 19

Conclusion 21

Disclaimer 23

Introduction To Amazon Free Time Unlimited

As parents, we often are concerned and sometimes upset when our kids spend lots of their time in front of their gadgets instead of spending it on books, encyclopedias, and other things that would expose them to a learning environment. In reality and in today's day and age, there are in fact countless educational resources online that can be helpful and contributed to our kids education and entertainment. We all know that children books like The Little Mermaid, The Three Musketeers, and Harry Potter, that have all once been a part of our childhood days, are now made available as eBooks, and even entire encyclopedias are readily available to our kids. Whether its browsing Google Maps, listening to Spotify, or perusing YouTube, our kids have ready access to education and entertainment—at times seemingly too much!

These platforms all have shortcomings too. YouTube, for example, has advertisements, which may appear on the screen once to thrice per video. The same goes with providers like Spotify which allows you to access its premium content and take out the advertisements only when you pay for a month or a year of subscription. This doesn't even scratch the surface of the enormous problem of a child happening upon adult-only content.

This is where Amazon FreeTime Unlimited enters the ring. It is a subscription service that gives kids an access to over 13,000 learning resources, including books, apps, games, and videos, that are compatible on Fire, Android, iOS and Kindle devices. It offers low prices and decent discounts for all its features and it is a great value even if you are already subscribed to Amazon Prime. Backed up with trusted sources, FreeTime Unlimited does not only limit itself to just providing an online learning environment for your child but also in making it secure and conducive so your child really does learn as they consume content. Included in the package as well are parental control features that are essential in keeping your kids aware of their time and avoid problematic situations, such as skipping their bedtimes because they're looking at a screen.

This book, then will cover all the features offered by Amazon FreeTime Unlimited, along with added information you might need, including the price breakdown, comparisons, subscription cancelling, and troubleshooting so you can maximize your subscription.

What is Amazon FreeTime Unlimited?

FreeTime Unlimited is an Amazon subscription service geared towards kids aged 3 to 12. FreeTime Unlimited offers access to thousands of child-friendly resources including books, shows, films, games, and apps from trusted brands like Disney and Nickelodeon. A large proportion of these resources for kids are available for free. Plus, your child can enjoy a huge number of all those resources without necessarily being fed an endless stream of advertisements. The service is personalized to each child's experience, which is the main reason why it is equipped with options to help your child explore new ideas and let them watch it the way they want to. Moreover, since kids are restricted to access social media or internet while in FreeTime, they are barred from making any in-app purchases.

A comfort for parents

FreeTime Unlimited includes very useful parental control features, which allows you to monitor their screen activity and their access to these different learning resources. Among these features is the Parent Dashboard, which allows you to review the books, videos, apps, and games your kids enjoy in FreeTime. Aside from that feature, it also allows you to manage settings, which include adding content from your personal library, restricting access to web browser, setting passwords to prevent unapproved app exits, pausing the device, and much more.

FreeTime Unlimited also gets you to limit your child's screen time, which can be challenging without the proper tools. With FreeTime, you can set usage time limits and even restrict access to certain categories, like videos and games, but also then you can allow your child to spend an unlimited time for reading simultaneously. In addition to the Parent Dashboard, FreeTime also has an age filter feature, which ensures age-appropriate content for your child within its space. Despite the fact that video offerings in this Amazon service seem to mirror what we already have seen on Roku and other platforms, it still remains a useful feature given the fact that parents are provided with options to tailor their child's experience.

FreeTime Unlimited also works great especially for parents who like to set educational goals for their kids. In fact, it has the "Learn First" feature reserved for parents to block their child's access to games, cartoons, and short videos, until their child has met educational goals for a certain time period. For parents who wanted to separate the contents viewed by their older kids and preschoolers, FreeTime has the option to create individual child profiles and give each of them selected access to the learning resources from their personal library. In that way, it's like having each kid own a personalized tablet or mobile device.

A portable service

While FreeTime Unlimited is mostly associated with the Fire tablets, customers can actually access it across a number of compatible devices including Echo, Kindle, iOS, and Android. Because each device has a different range of specs and limitations, there are also differences with regards to how much access and features are given when using a particular device. For example, an audio-based device like Echo Dot brings FreeTime Unlimited in the form of ad-free radio stations, podcasts, and audible books, which kids can access for hundreds of hours. With this package, parents are given access to the standard parental control features, including usage time limits, activity monitoring, and Smart Home setting management. Echo Dot Kids Edition comprises a year of FreeTime Unlimited subscription, a kid-friendly case, and a two-year warranty. Suffice it to say each individual device may have slightly different features available, but the vast majority of the important features are available on ALL devices regardless of manufacturer.

With Fire tablets, on the other hand, kids are provided access to a wider range of resources including popular apps, games, books, audible books, and videos from trusted kid-favorite sources like PBS Kids, Nickelodeon, and Disney. Aside from the standard parental control features, it also comes with the Amazon Parent Dashboard, which parents can use to set educational goals, limit their child's access to certain categories, and manage web browsing. With the same dashboard, parents can also impose screen time limits and monitor the resources viewed by their child. The Fire Kids Edition Tablet comprises a year of FreeTime Unlimited subscription, a kid-proof case, and a two-year warranty.

FreeTime Unlimited is also incorporated in a different way when using Amazon Kindle, this time in the form electronic books and reading materials. Basically, Kindle are a series of e-readers designed for users to browse, buy, download, and read e-books, newspapers, magazines and other digital content via wireless networking to the Kindle Store. With FreeTime, however, kids are already provided with thousands of these resources, including their all-time favorites such as Harry Potter, Pete the Cat, and Curious George. For each book, they can view their reading progress and track their reading accomplishments per day. Plus, kids can be motivated to read more as they are presented achievement badges each time they reach a reading milestone.

Included in the package are tools and features that allows parents to bar their kids from inappropriate content or websites, make unapproved purchases, and access to social media sites.

Using FreeTime along with iOS and Android devices offers almost the same benefits as that of using a Fire tablet. Kids are granted an access to more than 10,000 popular apps, games, videos, and books from Nickelodeon, Disney, PBS Kids, and more. Plus, the package also comes with the Amazon Parent Dashboard to monitor your child's screen activity. In addition to those standard features, the Discussion Card feature is enabled for these particular devices, giving the parents the ability to learn more about the titles of the learning resources taken by their child and gives guidance on conversation starters to help them connect and interact with their parents.

How it works

FreeTime Unlimited, with a year's subscription, will work across all your devices. So even if your kids are on an Android device, iOS smartphone, Kindle, or compatible Echo devices, you'll still retain the same amount of monthly or yearly subscription fee, which basically starts at less than three bucks a month. As mentioned before, you are also provided with a hands-on dashboard, which provide parental control features, which include setting of educational goals, imposing time regulations, controlling your kid's access to some learning resources, and pausing the device in times of meals and other family moments.

FreeTime Unlimited also promotes a kid-friendly browsing experience by blocking inappropriate content and allowing you, as a parent, to manage their web activities. In fact, while in FreeTime, the background color of the device changes to blue, which allows parents to know at a glance that their child is given off an age appropriate content. Furthermore, kids can only browse titles that have been selected for them through the parent dashboard.

FreeTime customers are also given the options to cancel a free trial or monthly subscription at any time through visiting its official website.

Prices and Deals

How much FreeTime costs depends on three things. First, whether or not you are an Amazon Prime member. Second, whether you pay on a monthly or an annual basis. Third, whether or not your subscription is limited just for a single child or a family of up to four children. On a monthly basis, FreeTime normally costs around five bucks for a single child and around ten dollars for two or more kids. This decreases to $2.99 USD for a Prime member subscribing for a single child and $6.99 USD for two or more kids. Opting for a yearly FreeTime subscription saves a lot of money especially if you have more than one child. While non-members pay $119 USD for a yearly prepaid plan, Prime members could save to as much as $36 USD if they choose that same membership.

The bottom line here is that Amazon Prime members receive a significant discount on FreeTime Unlimited. And, although Prime is expensive, I've gathered the top five ways to reliably get ***discounted Amazon Prime membership****!* If you <u>click on this link</u> I'll send you these sure-fire ways to get a discount on Amazon Prime with ALSO gives you FreeTime at a huge discount!

That link again: <u>Discount Amazon Prime</u>

Amazon Prime members are often given number of discounts and deals that are available when they are new FreeTime subscribers. In fact, during a recent discount period which has ended on August this year, Amazon gave 40% off a year of the FreeTime prepaid plan.

It is also important to know that Amazon regularly offers a free month-long trial, which is cancellable any time and are times when they offer a three-month subscription trial only for 99 cents.

Amazon also throws a year of its subscription service with every purchase of its own exclusive devices, including Echo, Kindle, and Fire. The current prices set for these devices usually start from as low as $80 USD. These prices are relatively lower as compared to the amount paid by non-Prime members by subscribing to a year worth prepaid plan, which is already included upon the purchase of these devices.

Similar Competitor Services

Amazon does really good in tailoring its product and services to particular needs of its market, which includes FreeTime Unlimited. There are competitors out there, however, and in this chapter, we'll be taking a look at FreeTime Unlimited and how it stands out or lags behind similar competitor services.

Google Family Link

Similar to FreeTime, Google's recently released Family link app is reserved for children under 13 years old and allows parents to set digital ground rules to guide them as they explore online. It allows parents to create separate Google accounts for each child, complete with access to most Google services. With Family Link, parents are made to help their children in making healthy decisions about what they do in their device by viewing their screen activities, managing their apps, and feeding their curiosity. Much like with how the Amazon Parent Dashboard works, Family Link also has a feature that allows parents to set usage time limits and lock a supervised device whenever it's time to go play outside, have dinner, or spend time together.

Like Amazon, Google requires a download of the Family Link app to setup parental controls within your kid's device. However, when using Family Link, you still need to create a separate email account for your child and go through the setup process, where you'll need two devices on Nougat or later Android versions. Amazon, on the other hand, does not need you to create an email account for your child, but instead you are just required to link their profile to your existing Amazon account. After the setup has been finished, you can easily manage their account on the web from any device you are using, however you have to visit the official Amazon website.

In terms of compatibility, both Google and Amazon assume that their users are not only using the devices that they are exclusively providing.

Google, for example, reserves its Family Link app for both Android and iOS devices. While it's great, it does not mean it can win against FreeTime in this particular category provided that the latter is already covering up these two adaptive platforms plus three devices that are provided by Amazon, namely Kindle, Fire, and Echo.

Inside the two parental control apps, you can find a lineup of toggles, switches, and dials that allows you to control how long you want your child to be exposed in front of their device for a day. Once the allotted time you have set eventually gets used up, the device will immediately notify your child that they can no longer use it. While Amazon Freetime divides its time into weekdays and weekends rather than individuals days, Family Link on the other hand, allows you to set a total screen time per day. This is among the major upper hand for Family Link against FreeTime since the latter does not provide each day its own toggle, which makes it difficult for you to adjust during a holiday or a special event.

Despite being an important feature, both Google and Amazon devices don't have any kill switch included. However, you still have the *Pause Devices* in FreeTime and the *Lock Now* feature in Family link to instantly shut your kid's device down. FreeTime gives you an hour to twelve shutdown period, while Family Link shuts your device until the next day's bed time. Both shutdown methods can be overridden especially if you change your mind and shift the shutdown time to what you think that is most appropriate for your child. While both are simple and easy, Freetime appears to be more convenient, especially in choosing time intervals, as compared to Family Link's all-or-nothing option.

Screen Time

Although it might sound like FreeTime's sister subscription service, Screen Time is actually an iOS software made with the same purpose of monitoring and controlling what kids do with their device. Similar with Google Family Link, Screen Time as of the date exists for further testing and is expected to come soon to an iPad or iPhone along with the introduction of Apple's iOS 12. Screen Time works by telling you how long your kids have been using certain apps on your device and allowing you to place numerous app usage limits for them. The software's digital controls include more menus, buttons, and bar charts, which details out how often your child has been using the device and provides you a percentage of time spent on specific categories like Social Networking, Games, and Productivity.

Screen Time comes with the "Downtime" feature, which is similar to setting up bedtime mode for your phone. Downtime works by shutting down your kid's phone for a specific number of time, only allowing access to calls and kid-friendly apps that are greenlighted. Parents are given the options as to when they want to shut down their child's device and turn it back on again. This feature is particularly useful if you want to keep your children from skipping their bedtimes looking at their screen or lock the device during family times like meals, trips, and special occasions.

This may sound promising but iOS users looking for help from this new Apple feature might be surprised at the end of the day. First, despite having Apple well aware of the fact that this is to be used by parents, has the default setting set to adult content. Unlike Amazon's FreeTime, whose child safety features are already set by the time of subscription, iOS default settings seem to work the opposite way. Explicit content is left unrestricted by default and there are no available privacy protection system installed within the device. You can remotely change these settings and approve media purchases, but it will eventually require more time and work.

Second, compared with FreeTime Unlimited, Screen Time has also a lot of loopholes especially in setting up a usage time limit. If your kid has to ever watch a video on Netflix and long press the home button to make it appear as a picture-in-picture, the Screen Time limit you have set won't count against them. Chances are, they can watch it all day long without having you monitor their activity during that time. Apple also allows your child to request time extensions, which constantly pops up as a notification and gather in big chunks that is quite annoying.

Last, the biggest benefit to Amazon FreeTime Unlimited as compared to Family Link and Screen Time is its year's worth of access to thousands of apps, games, videos, books, and other learning resources from top kid-friendly brands. It has all that content curated, most ads removed, and has restricted as well the access to social media sites to avoid any in-app purchases. None of those things, so far, were included as features in Family Link and Screen Time. Moreover, unlike a single user based device like iOS 12, Amazon devices are made to be shared by parents and multiple siblings, with each individual profiles assigned and tailored according to their ages.

FamilyTime

FamilyTime is a Tokyo-based parental control app, which allows you to manage all your child's devices in a secure, remote manner. It includes a number of features including a daily app limit, screen time scheduling, SafeSearch and Internet filters, app blocker, and location tracker. Apart from its standard security features, it also comes with a "Pick Me Up" feature for your children to let you know when and where to pick them up from through the press of a single button. Setting up FamilyTime app is very easy and only takes a few minutes to complete.

Along with its promising qualities, FamilyTime is much cheaper when compared to a year of non-member family FreeTime subscription that shaves off more or less 120 dollars in a single prepaid plan. FamilyTime plans are based on the number of devices, which works totally opposite with FreeTime Unlimited that mostly depends on the number of children subscribed to the service. One FamilyTime license enough for a single device goes for around $27 USD per year, while two licenses amount to just 35 dollars. Going all out with five licenses will only cost you around $69 USD, which is 70% lesser than the cost you can come in for if you are a non-Amazon member and you go all out with its year worth of FreeTime subscription service.

While Amazon FreeTime is available only as a single app, FamilyTime covers a more streamlined approach. That is, there are two FamilyTime apps on the Google Play Store, one reserved for the parents to monitor their kid's screen activity and one reserved for children, to have themselves tracked with everything they do in front of their gadget screens. While the parent app only requires logging into your FamilyTime account; the child app, on the other hand, requires you to provide basic information including your name, date of birth, and relation (son or daughter). After filling up these things up, you have to click on the *Activate Button* and enable various permissions to begin using the service.

Unlike FreeTime, there are some FamilyTime features, such as Geofencing alerts, that only work with Wi-Fi or cellular connection. What is even more concerning is the fact that a child can easily uninstall the software without your approval. In order to prevent this from happening, you have to discuss to your kid the importance of using a mobile phone or tablet safely and try to negotiate with them some time.

Troubleshooting

FreeTime Unlimited is another page in the success story of Amazon. It all started with the original Kindle Unlimited, and changed over time as Amazon went into an upgrade and renovated its Android services. Although FreeTime has been constantly receiving positive responses from its customers, we cannot deny the fact that even the most renowned subscription services carry along some downsides with them. Beyond being available to only a few compatible devices and having some shortcomings with regards to the software itself, there are a few common FreeTime issues you may encounter. Listed below are solutions and workarounds to help you get past through them.

Items that are free are limited or the "light" versions, and often require in-app purchases that are very hard to track once you've bought them.

Make sure that your device is registered to the correct Amazon account. If you're using Household profiles, verify that you have signed in for a correct profile to track such items that you have just recently purchased, as some of them might not appear in child profiles. Swipe down from the top of the screen, scroll through the app settings, and tap *My Account*. If you see a wrong account listed, deregister the account and sign in using the correct account.

If the parent buys an app, it may be available under the parent's profile, but not under their kids' – even if you have it set to deliver to the kid.

It is important for you to take note that only you or another adult in your household can purchase an app, and add or remove them in Amazon FreeTime. Your child can open and use these items so long as you have added them onto their separate profile.

To add content to a child profile:

1. Swipe down from the top of your device's screen and tap *Settings*. Scroll through *Profiles & Family Library*, enter the lock

screen password, and then tap *Add content to a child profile*. You can also perform this within your child's profile by doing the same.

2. Proceed to your child's profile and tap *Manage Child's Content*. From there, you can tick the checkbox next to each title of the items you want to add to your child's profile. To take out some items, you'll just have to uncheck the boxes again.

As a tip, you can tap the *For Kids* option to view recommended kid-friendly titles and have them incorporated into your personal library.

If the parent did buy an app and were able to get it on their kids' profile, they may not be able to play it because the app is "not allowed" on FreeTime.

In some cases, purchased and downloaded content are shown as locked and may not be able to play when accessing the app through FreeTime. When this happens, immediately log into your child's FreeTime Unlimited account and try doing a restore of past purchases.

Cancelling FreeTime: How do you make sure it is canceled so the parent doesn't keep getting charged for it?

To completely unsubscribe from Amazon FreeTime Unlimited on your device:

1. Hover through the *Manage Content & Subscription* tab from the *Parent Settings*.
2. Key in the password for your parent account.
3. In the same tab, select the *Unsubscribe from Amazon FreeTime Unlimited* option.

You may also use the Parent Dashboard to unsubscribe to the service. Just go to FreeTime's official website, to submit and confirm your cancellation.

When the parent does finally decide to cancel FreeTime, will their kids' profiles be wiped?

After unsubscribing from FreeTime Unlimited, you will be given a full refund to cover your most recent subscription charge. While any content from your subscription will no longer be accessible, items you have purchased and added to your child's profile will still be available.

Subscription Process and Setup

FreeTime Unlimited is a monthly all-in-one subscription that automatically updates with each purchase of a Fire Kids Edition tablet or a Kindle Fire reader. In order to use or renew your subscription, you'll need a current, valid payment method in your Amazon account. Also take note that the resources available in FreeTime refreshes each time you subscribe to this particular service. You can access your subscription through any supported devices registered to the same account.

To begin your subscription while browsing on your Fire, Echo, or Kindle devices (note: you can do this on Amazon's site as well, which is described later on):

1. Visit the system settings. Under the *Profiles & Family Library* options, hover to your child's profile and the select *Subscribe to Amazon FreeTime Unlimited*.
2. You'll then be prompted to select a monthly subscription plan, which is divided into two specific prepaid subscriptions, namely single child and family plans. The former covers only a single child registered to the subscription service while the latter covers up to four children in your household.
3. If you are an Amazon Prime member, you are eligible to avail for a discounted monthly plan. Just visit the official website to see details about FreeTime's current pricing.

If you are planning to subscribe outside of Fire, Echo, and Kindle devices, simply go to the Amazon website and start the process. New members are eligible for a month of free trial and will be subject to the monthly charges should they fail to cancel their subscription at the end of the trial period.

FreeTime content will soon appear in your child's profile after your device has been connected to a wireless network. You can download any content onto your device in case you want thr resources available without an internet access.

To initiate FreeTime on your device, tap *Settings* and proceed to the *Profiles & Family Library* tab. Access to the *Add Child Profile* screen by tapping *Add Child*. Complete the necessary details and add a profile photo. After filling up the background information, you'll be prompted with an option to select between *Amazon FreeTime* and *Teen Profiles*.

Amazon FreeTime profile is reserved for children ages eight and younger. It locks the device to portrait orientation, which is a perfect setup in case you want them to scroll through picture books and other available learning resources. Teen profiles on the other hand are available for children nine years and older, which is still backed up by the same security and protection of the Amazon FreeTime profile.

Tap *Add Profile* and begin selecting for content titles to add from your personal library. Save all settings by simply tapping *Done* to finish the setup process.

Conclusion

Amazon FreeTime Unlimited is an excellent tool for today's busy parents. If you're like most parents and prefer the idea of having some firm ground rules with regards to your child's electronic experience, then there's no reason for you not to subscribe to this family-oriented Amazon service as it allows you easy control over your child's exposure to electronic content. Aside from the standard benefits you can get when you subscribe, you can also take an advantage of a year worth FreeTime subscription if you purchase a Kindle Fire HD.

If you liked this book and found it helpful, please leave a review of it on Amazon by following this link: https://www.amazon.com/dp/B07L7WJVQZ

Disclaimer

All attempts have been made to verify the information contained in this book but the authors and publisher do not bear any responsibility for errors or omissions. Any perceived negative connotation of any individual, group, or company is purely unintentional. Furthermore, this book is intended as a guide and as such, any and all responsibility for actions taken upon reading this book lies with the reader alone and not with the author or publisher. Additionally, it is the reader's responsibility alone and not the author's or publisher's to ensure that all applicable laws and regulations for business practice are adhered to. Lastly, we sometimes utilize affiliate links in the content of this book and as such, if you make a purchase through these links, we will gain a small commission. We have used each of the services listed in this book, however, and as such we can say that we would recommend them to our closest friends with the same ease that we now recommend them to you.

Copyright © 2018 by Creative Dynamics, LLC